Bitter English

AHMAD ALMALLAH

Bitter English

THE UNIVERSITY OF CHICAGO PRESS

Chicago and London

The University of Chicago Press, Chicago 60637
The University of Chicago Press, Ltd., London
© 2019 by The University of Chicago
All rights reserved. No part of this book may be used or reproduced in any manner
whatsoever without written permission, except in the case of brief quotations
in critical articles and reviews. For more information, contact the University of
Chicago Press, 1427 East 60th Street, Chicago, IL 60637.
Published 2019
Printed in the United States of America

28 27 26 25 24 23 22 21 20 19   1 2 3 4 5

ISBN-13: 978-0-226-64264-2 (paper)
ISBN-13: 978-0-226-64278-9 (e-book)
DOI: https://doi.org/10.7208/chicago/9780226642789.001.0001

Library of Congress Cataloging-in-Publication Data

Names: Almallah, Ahmad Y., author.
Title: Bitter English / Ahmad Almallah.
Other titles: Phoenix poets.
Description: Chicago ; London : The University of Chicago Press, 2019. |
    Series: Phoenix poets | Includes bibliographical references.
Identifiers: LCCN 2018054730 | ISBN 9780226642642 (pbk. : alk. paper) |
    ISBN 9780226642789 (e-book)
Subjects: LCSH: Almallah, Ahmad Y.—Poetry. | Palestinian Arabs—Poetry. |
    Palestinian Americans—Poetry. | Immigrants—United States—Poetry. |
    Identity (Psychology)—Poetry. | LCGFT: Poetry. | Autobiographical poetry.
Classification: LCC PS3601.L573 B57 2019 | DDC 811/.6—dc23
LC record available at https://lccn.loc.gov/2018054730

♾ This paper meets the requirements of ANSI/NISO Z39.48-1992
(Permanence of Paper).

For Nawal

and only our dreams have not been humiliated

Zbigniew Herbert

CONTENTS

ACKNOWLEDGMENTS

Many thanks to the following journals and magazines in which earlier versions of these poems first appeared:

> *Apiary*: "Bookcase"
> *Michigan Quarterly Review*: "House Cleaning"
> SAND: "Citizenship Interview"

To my first readers: my partner, Huda Fakhreddine, and my daughter, Samaa.

And to Michael Collier and Tom Sleigh, for reading many versions of these poems and for all their encouragement and support.

BITTER ENGLISH

that I own no one language cuts me through
that I find this english tongue I use day after day
boring, in construction, even in poetry, cuts me
in the middle of sentiment and sentence

I do not understand this sound, I stumble
as I say to myself I will ignore these english words
emptied today, I walk down the street catching
my hand in the air, greeting faces I know I don't know

as I walk these streets only owning past echoes
cutting through this language, this english tongue
I want to catch with my teeth cuts me through

that I have to stack all my old and new passports
on my writing cuts me through—I go over
my exits and entries for this citizenship, my first
step, I doubt, to owning something of this sound

I owe everything to one place that owns me, not
here, where what I owe I do not own, time and many
years spared because this english tongue cuts me
through, because this english tongue owes me

a language

I

Rites of Passage

CITIZENSHIP INTERVIEW

An order
is an order
yes I get it—
I do

not

understand:
He tells me
to raise
the voice

mine

to answer
loudly
clearly:
Yes I get

it

I do—no
longer
understand
an order—

is

yes:

an order—
so I will
leave my

pass-

ports
there
for your
pair of

exam-

ining
eyes
there—
on the

edge

of this
pressed
wood—
while you

do

whatever
you are
now
doing—

and

while
you are
at it
I'll cross

my

legs
in front
of your
officer

face:

To show
you the
sheen
of my

ceremonial
black
shoes.

JISR

1

In the air, in the plane, in the opening
of dark wounds:

I hold both in one hand, which one
should I use,

I hold both in one hand, American
blue
       passport,

or this thing "Palestinian Authority"
inscribed

in
        gold

and marred
     and stained
         by its own
            color.

["To the bridge?" the Jordanian
officer asks—
     rhetorical man
     stamping my Palestinian
Authority
       passport:

And on the escalator down
        a piano
                and a player

in the middle of this
revolving

        progress.]

2

In the taxi, on the way to land
control,

I talk nothing of that sort
I only
                        stare
at the uneventful fall
                        out of a pane
covered with warm dust
                        and disdain:
How green it all is
                        still

how olive are the fields.

[Only in case, I hide the American
blue,
        only
in
    case

I get held up
        somehow:

And how mistaken I was
        when digging
        out old things and times
        bad purchases and
        indecision
                waiting for

this package
        —a passport—

        for my new American
        life
        in my
garage I said:

        After this
        there will be
        nothing
on the mind.]

3
The land could take you there by
its own accord,
the divided pie is being warmed
up
        in the October meditations

                of sun.

[And father's words

I
     remember
     a distant
unknown reality:

"Amman to Bethlehem,"
he said,
"before all this
     a two-hour
car ride."]

4
It's dark now waiting
I've only
     known Jericho at this hour
                    waiting:
And leaning against
               a yellow
van with the driver
               blowing
smoke

     and complaining
     of the dearth
     of passengers

          to Bethlehem.

[It's considered a "rest-area"
     it's named.
It's full of vehicles that take
and take

and take:
Buses of people
coming to the Palestinian
side,
        after crossing
        on another
        bus
from Jordan
        to the Israeli
side,

the drained stream
that once was
        a
Jordan River.]

5
We buckle up on settlement,

we see the sign "Jerusalem"

we go the other way, to where

        we avoid—

we never go through:

Always the side roads, always
the rough edges of hills, to
the ups and downs
        where Palestinian
        towns
around this holy city

move with the sound
and call
of this
        "valley
              of fire."

[And as soon as we get a chance
out of settlement roads,
        we unbuckle
this body destined
        to ruin.]

6
The sides of this van
this vehicle to
        Bethlehem
                all
senses:

The call to prayer, the butcher
meat, the blood and bones,
the car, the lots, and the open
engine:
        And the air brushing
the hand and hair:
        The slope
the incline, the swerve
                and bump:
And after the checkpoint,
the sweets shop in the middle

        of nowhere.

[And today at check,
      a point
          a wave
but at times a wait
and at others
      the questions
take.]

7
In the mind all wire and stone.

[And in memory
the iron rusting and
      railing
green

      leaves.]

8
On this island, in the middle
of the road—
         how did
the vehicle make it
      up this incline:
Out
     the valley
     of fire—
the Palestinian Authority
officer

waving death.

[It's the end of round-
abouts,
     the way around
Jerusalem:
     And up that
hill

     after the officer

if there was light

the dome of the rock

shines

in many

eyes.]

9
We are approaching
I say:

"You'd have to back it
up
     —your van—
the only
     way
         out
of this narrow road."

"It's OK," he

says.

[I did
        forget
I do
        remind
my
        self
how
        forgetful
I am.]

By the iron door that's
now green,
        I remember
                its old
beige and brown.

"Stop here," suddenly I say:

He brakes—

        we step out:

He unloads
my
        small bag:

I take out my wallet

and pay him

in a different

currency.

[And here I am

     forgetful
     and remembering
     and dusting
     off the winds

at

     last.]

MAP

         From above
we pass
     the places
I couldn't visit on this return:

         It's all there
         on the screen
         in front of me

   and for me
      to see—
only on a screen.

I look out window-
panes:
     Yes,

we're above clouds,
nothing recognizable
    from Amman, we
    pass
over more white clouds—

over Jerusalem now—

    I turn the screen to
language:
    Are these Arabic
words I see?

Why . . .
I can't read them anymore:

Maybe
    —I say—
        maybe

    I need

to be there

    on level
        with land

    in order

to read
    the land.

II

House

PICTURES

we sat together you and I mother next to son
the armchairs worn against the dullness of white walls
you read aloud the same sentence over and over

I place your hand in mine do I let go I stand
there was between us something everything
to you the past is us the past the past is everything

and there I look the beige cupboard full of pictures
it's still closed up your youth I know almost nothing
I am your son the youngest one the son of your aging

I open up the beige the black and white pictures
your arms revealed and in the sun revealing
the weak and slender hand is aimless on the table

I place a photo in your palm your daughter and your sons
I am a child the funny face I make you point to him
you ask if he belongs to me I say he is your son

you do not know you look at me in wonder
the past the past is everything the present
your mind the nerves the stems of blood bursting

THE HOUSE

I

Is there an earliest memory I can go back to? I don't know exactly what to go back to. I vaguely see a scene from a house we used to rent, not very far away from what became to me "the house," "the first place," "the beginning of it all"—which turns out just now, by the turn of these sentences, not to be the first. Not very strange, we live imagining the facts . . . and now I can see shadowy female figures sitting together in a living room, in that house we rented before "the house," the one I remember my mother calling *dar al-haj*. I can also see now a particular female figure, maybe in her late twenties, with long, thick black hair, and I can hear my mother telling me of her finding me so incredibly edible that she bit my ear.

II

I think. One of the earliest memories from the place that became our house is the huge, deep pit that lay behind it. We had this door at the back of "the house" that opened up to this hole in the earth. I remember my father opening that door not necessarily to show me anything and I happened to be there, playing in an unfinished kitchen, and I saw it. The pit was finally turned into a well that collects the rainwater from the house's flat roof, and I'm not sure if my uncle and his wife and kids moved into that level of the house before or after the construction of the well. But I do remember the iron door there that remained closed for a very long time.

III

Was it my father or my mother who kept talking and repeating the story of moving into the house before installing any windows? My father told the story as a proof of my mother's stubbornness. She wouldn't stay to pay another month's rent while there was a house that was now hers, a short walk away. How unsettled she must've been . . . and this just occurs to me. She wanted to move in at once, make the place her own. It didn't make a difference if there were windows installed or not. Though I never could imagine or figure out whether the iron railings covering the openings in the structure we eventually called windows were installed or not. They must've installed the main iron door to move in there. Can it be . . . and my mother must've known it, that what constituted the house is that door, which locked a portion of her world inside a structure.

IV

A feeling kept me above the ground all the time. What calls this hunger? Every time I put down a sentence, I think of all the details to negate it.

LINES OF RETURN

I   Give me one hint, give me the thing that is spark, stop
telling me that I should no longer lie to myself, I know
I look ridiculous holding onto this memory or that, trying
to stare myself down, as I repeat the lines: you are not
you, you are you, done with, over. Strange you are at
home, in this house of fact, this house of ruin: you are
you, looking past the laundry line on the roof, at the hills
as all flames have to be put off, as the sun goes down, as
the time is so obvious. There is no one, none: we gather
ourselves inside, we flatten thoughts on the rugs praying:
mother, on this couch repeating sounds, bowing, are you?

II   At the sight of ruins, stop. They're tearing
it down, the old theater knocked in half, sliced
like cake, for everyone to gape at the empty
layers, all the way to the back, against the
last wall standing: the stairs with the iron
railings swaying rusty branches and leaves.
Say something to the empty seats hanging
in everyone's view like charms: everyone's
memory is here. Walk away, don't look in,
inside, this is your blind spot, this is where you
split the atoms of disaster, this is where you
draw lines on lines on lines, this is where you
reach out for the lemon tree's fruit, this is
where you recall the hand pricked by thorns.

III   When I was a child I was always, dear mother, on you
                                   depending:
       I followed you up these stairs, and you set no
                       law,
       just song. We walked the stairs together and we had nothing to
                       ground
       us in the land but the hands we held against air.
                       See
       how you reach for the grape leaves hanging against the rust
                       there,
       see how the stones keeping the dirt from collapsing are also
                       railing.

HOUSE CLEANING

(1. kitchen)

there is a lot to take cleaning a kitchen   first of all there is the dead mouse
or is it dead asleep   no sound I make then
banging around   no movement

nothing

and what is the best way to pick up dead things   out
of the windowpanes   father and son walking
and talking   yes   there is a lot to take cleaning a kitchen and looking for the source
I open up cabinets filled with things that look back
funny old food   how old   how long ago   how many times did I bring
the same thing   wrapped the same wrap   used the same old plastic   hanging
by the rotten kitchen door   yes same   we did it together at times   always now
is never   and my mother my mother   my mother she   wrapping everything
   seeds and feeds   sumac   many bags wrapped in bags   packed and stacked

one
on top of the other   many more there
wrapped over the years

forgotten

and opening up the abyss of a black trash bag   the cleaning starts   small
bags dropping into the big bag   and the hand
     that handles

hesitates

(2. garden)

as I was raking dead leaves in my city garden in philly   and upon finding the broken
    tip of an iron tool   used to pick the ground and dig out dirt   I realized I
    know nothing of the terminology for the things and tools of the earth
            in this english tongue I use every day   composing and raking leaves
                I am what I am   a deserter of my own language unsheathing
    the sword of otherness   it begins cutting   my disdain   for the
    adoption and the pitiful thing adopted and the whip   lashing out against
    the world   and how have you been doing this a.m.   well
    historically speaking I've been part of the disadvantaged of the earth all my life
    and for seventeen years now   I've been bottling up selves   and sticking
    plastic bottles   in the best of
american frigidaires

THE HUNT, A HOME
for Diya

I
In front of the house, a broken tile:
    part of the past order—

it reminds me of the Egyptian man who owned
the place:
    a hoarder
    of dark wood,
of the black
    stuff
    that lodges itself on skin beneath the eye,
    and what
    is it about the rusty

brown
    of a broken tile that sums it all? I don't know,
    I don't remember
        much

of what he had, but all his years in exile were there,
                in that
    house,
        and on top

of the old tile that I can see now
            staring at me,
    he "installed"
    a newer kind

    a bright color for time.

My brother and I walk
his steps
noticing how every-

thing was kept, how everything,
a cover—how can
this man move out of this place?

How and where
is he going to store all his years?

II

The street is being blocked:
    a car
    is backing up
    in the

middle of the road.
    How could they—I look—transport a whole
    house? In this space

the roots are malleable and the uprootedness
                          not really
    the thing at hand, it

is the thing at work—

I imagine a tree in place of the house,
             its roots dangling on

pavement,
    brushing against the cold April winds
    as the "over-
    sized load" signs, with

the flashing cars from the front and back
              pass the entire
    block
by, and I see windows

passing me by   and I look down

to where the wheels roll   away
    the whole house:
lo and behold!

There are no roots dangling from this
        wood:

        only the air making

the rounds
                of a gone by time.

III

And hear again! This is how the story goes:
in this country,
in these parts of land   it's

all about this wood   that wants to gather
          all the elements of its
          end.

And long ago
                    my brother meets
          the light in his name,

in a word,
                    and the light travels fast.
                              Diya keeps running with
          that name, trying to

reflect the flame
                    within himself,
                    his true nature if you will
          but exile
                    catches up

with all his steps.
          He tries to settle and contain himself
          within a structure, of

mirrors, but everything freezes with the cold,
          and the waters in pipes

begin expanding beyond their means
and the solid quality

of the matter makes copper

burst, and then a trickle begins filling walls
with what-
      ever liquid escapes this
                    deadening
cold.
            Everything fills

and slowly the abandoned house makes
itself at home.

THE HOUSE, SEARCHED

i

The house, searched, is not something that gives way to form. My attempts to put it to some rhythm and sound always turn out to be laughable. At least for me.   I read what I put down in lines about it, and I can't take my own experience seriously. And I'm thinking, am I really wired in such a way to produce all these clichés of war, to reproduce all the images we've been seeing in movies   in the news? Why can't I take myself seriously? I'm experiencing a movie-like moment, some momentary empathy toward that boy I was, and then cut:

we're

in a different time and place, aren't we?

There is no need to fret
over disaster.

ii

My wife tells me of her own experience with house searches. She lived in the south   of Lebanon—

And it seems the protocol is one, standardized: a higher-ranking military officer leads the house search
ordering the door open   with a bang   not so to speak   walks in the house

accompanied by two soldiers   he brings out of his throat a broken kind of Arabic

talks to the head of the household with it   in a polite courteous manner   a real

  gentleman he was, my father said

    there is a curious exchange between him and his two soldiers   they want to rush to

conclusions   they want to take and break   but the polite officer begs them patience
restraint   talks sense into them   while other soldiers in the background are taking
apart everything, opening the closets, ripping the mattresses open with a blade sticking
    out of
their rifles   I won't use the words machine gun or M16   they sound way too
overdramatic   and regardless   one or two soldiers go up the stairs   to the roof—
    I've been through it but I don't remember any of it—   I'm merely comparing notes
here: what my father said   and what my wife is now telling me—

She gets animated   starts speeding up the pace of events   something
    inside her is stirring or being stirred   her face is suddenly flushed   she's getting
    tired of her own maneuvers at conveying—
                                        Why
                                        I want to laugh now.

THE BOOKCASE

1

After the eye can no longer take on the world,
vaguely, it looks vaguely, as though hidden
behind a shield of shadows, and after my last trip
to Palestine, I sit in Philly staring at the bookcase
in our living room, around me I keep seeing
mother's lips moving toward these words.
I couldn't then understand, when home, when
traveling back, one truth, pure emotion, no
calculation, this is the moment of anger:
                              "You are all waiting
for me to die. I want to go back to my mother."

2

After the eye can no longer take on the word,
after it sees its truth glaring, as though it's waking
up against the morning sun, remembering
all of this now, and how it happened so quickly:
I can't remember anything! I sit staring
at the bookcase in our living room, while my
daughter watches Arabic cartoons on TV.
I see the wood collecting everything but books:
time, how many times are being collected, and
all those books I picked up from side streets
in America . . . how did we survive all this moving?
How could anyone survive life without once
saying,
        "I want to go back to my mother."

3

After the eye can no longer take on the void,
after it sees nothing in truth, after it closes
its lid to the light, after disaster, after all . . .
we sit by the bookcase, I beside it, my wife
with her back to it, as we are trying: our
daughter stares at the moving images on TV,
smiles at them. My wife tells me I need to
see this video. She tells me I have to! And
where would I fit another image. Aren't we
                                      drowned?
Isn't the world just full? And those words
as
        the body
lies on shore for the waves to rock gently,
as I see the little dead boy sleeping, death
seeping, mothers crying, and the order, all
things disappearing, and us, lining up
against the sea and its waves shouting,
                            "You are all
waiting for me to die.
            I want to go back to my mother."

III

Mother in Between

MATTERS OF LIGHT, FOG, AND SOMETIMES SMOKE

i

The sudden warmth in the dead of cold cold winter has created the fog, that is the smoke, that is the dimmer of light. I'm looking at one ray of it, in the street, in the sky. I facilitate a mechanical pull on the blind. I see another ray, and there . . . another. Now I don't know what to make of all this—I mix sugar with simmering water under a light heat. I add the grind and start stirring clockwise and counter, and when I pour myself a cup, some rays of wrinkled light begin to grow out of a small thought: I call in the steam as the wind starts beating against the glass. And the eye can't help itself . . . it looks in all the wrong directions.

ii

The lights are dimmed in the coffee shop where I remain trapped in my own pretense. I try to look intelligent and contemplative lest I forget my position in front of the streams of steam that cover the windowpanes with fog. I'm waiting for the door to open, and in the meantime, I am eyeing my observations: there is a pipe that comes very close to my sight as I extend a thought to where it joins the roof, to where it gathers and collects whatever the weather offers. I hear a click announcing a visitor, I want to look but I see the weight of a drop pulling a line of clarity to what is out of view.

PONTIFICATE

i

the sun has already risen, a couple of days ago I woke up
with the clear pronunciation of the word: the way to stairs
pronounced it, the steps guided me to the door, can you
believe: everything *pontificate* . . . it was said in describing
my father, though it was inaccurate it was fitting and some-
how, I never noticed this brick wall on the side, here, of this
building, somehow it was pontificating, somehow it was:
this laying out of brick after brick, and like my father it was
taciturn, intentionally holding back and yes: *thank you*
you are welcome, yes we welcome you, our doors are
open to you and your daughter of course, ahlan wa sahlan . . .
how he turns to this grinding formality and what does he
want to prove and at what point of his life did he adopt
this form, and with it the formality of the classical Arabic
(not the tongue, not the language as I now think about it)?
And suddenly he is a scholar of the Arabic language, speak-
ing in a scholarly manner that most people found strange
and funny, and it was something: it hid his village accent . . .
then he was able to be humble with it, to feign, but who
am I to pontificate here on the matter, who am I but the
receiver of bad ends, but the edge of this burnt-out piece
of
    wire.

ii

this should go on as a matter of the fact, the title of it, this
life, this piece: yes the clear glass is surely clear, but not
now, not at this hour, not here at least, not with this
transparency, that's a sham, that, like all shams, needs
an audience: people looking with pupils, moving beyond
this clarity, into the fog, into the way and the road—
yes there are steps you take and steps you take, all the
way I think of you father, I talk about you to our guests,
we eat the food my mother used to make, the one now
I make, and when I fill the small pot with the water, with
the salty mix, we boil . . . I add more salt, I don't get angry—
I've already done that: and now this dissolving, now these
     specks
          making a mess.

CHRONOLOGY

i

How do you wrap your head
Around anything

    The hand turns the paper
    Cup
    Clockwise clockwise
    And counter
    Before the hot
    Sip

How do you wrap your head
Around that

    The squirrels chase
    Each other in spirals
    Around the wood
    The pole

He's the bad guy, that father—
Just like I turn out to be—

Sticking the pills on one
Tip of a banana
White, yellow, and green
Buttons
Barely visible
But there

46

He's the bad guy forcing it
Into her mouth
And quickly quickly
So she won't
Have time
     To spit
The pills
Out

He's the bad guy just like
I am
     But I
Angry impulsive
     Violet
     For no particular
Reason.

ii
I hear him in the night
Reading the Qur'an
What sustains him

3 a.m.

I hear him in the night
Calling a name . . .

A call to help, he
Knows and hears
I can't sleep

Yes what?

A call for help, how
Can he keep the mask
So tight

On his face?

iii
Right after the prayer
The last of day
A thud
      A scream

I'm thanking God
Allah
      That all
Is well

That all
          Will
Be

I end the call
      Heading
Up

The stairway
To where
      They are

Mother
Stretched on the floor
A body in silent

Pain
     Moaning
     Gently

Barely
A sound

I don't know
What?!

Dragging her
To bed
     She must
Have escaped
This body
This all

Control control
And
     Stretched
On the
     Floor

Waiting
     For hands
To cling
     To arms

Waiting
     To be

Pushed back
     To bed

I stay
    There

Pushing her head
Back
    To pillow

Stroking her hair
Cut so short

Reading to her
A chapter or two
Of small
    Holy words.

RECYCLING
for mother

i. plastic

it contains
surely—   everything is
and must   be
in place
contained

the things that come
        poured
                inserted
into what
suffocates—
no pores
no air
coming
in
        or out

and the sun
                brutal light
rays of sudden
        eyes
reflected
on glass
        piercing
without
killing

only light
coming through
only thing
piercing
into this
maybe.

ii. compost

every scrap of food
had to go
in whole
                every bit of food
the ground
        the earth   dirt
        and stone

        you ask me to dig a hole
        in the ground
for your composting
        down a few steps
I am slashing

        through air
        raising the pick
and landing it:
        earth collapsing
dirt and stone
pushed in
for the turn
        and the cut   widening

        and I

hearing the water
bubbling
underneath
vision

this pot
this boil

and no matter what—

no vinegar can—

stop these beets
from bleeding.

iii. cloth

the line: a metal wire

hands touching current

we take wet and hang
by making small

folds

all edges are bent now

and clip clip   fingers reaching
for colors
rattling and rattled
by touch:

the sun a sudden light
appearing at noon
from the concrete east:

you and I on roof hanging—
each piece belonging
only to each

and you patting us through
the wet and empty things
we wear

together the hands hang:
one by one
we left

and you by your hands
picking only what is
yours—

thank God you recall now
a nothing a pile: dirty clothes
sheets and covers left
untouched.

iv. waste

in your world nothing went

to waste   nothing

in your world   and joking once

I said to my American friend: my mother

in her world nothing went to waste

—you the world's best recycler—   laughing
how so

but nothing went to waste
                              your hands
setting things aside
                    for wild cats

saving bread for birds

and the chickens in the backyard
ate everything you said

and the skin gentle hands getting coarse

picking out
zucchini hearts   setting them aside

on stove
              the heat
                              underneath
cooking

water   coming out of faucet

saved by the pot for plants

in your world   one kind

only one pair of shoes

you clung to.

v. snow

and the pile of snow in the middle
of the square

almost

         gone

and the screams in the middle

    of night

almost

         gone

    mama
mama

the cold that has turned drops
into hard flakes

almost

gone

and the warm air   brushing

against the pile of snow

in the middle of the square

melting
melting

—all what is left

now
                    lines

and edges

that days ago
held snow.

INTO HIS OWN

I keep getting these messages from you, father,
these texts, with prayers, implorations to Allah
with flowers . . . roses in the background, written
calligraphically and decoratively in the most
broken Arabic—what happened to your deep
regard for the holy and complicated science

of Arabic grammar? Is this the sign of the world
now? Yes I read them, those texts, and I want to
laugh, though I'm crying out to you now father:
what is it with you and disaster? It's some sort of
bad fiction, unbelievable, beyond any customary

imagination—nothing to stir sympathy or solidarity,
only doubt: Is this shit for real? Of course you wouldn't
like that, you turn away from probing masks. You
want us near and distant—what can I say to you?
restlessly standing by a mother losing her mind.

People do imagine disasters they can't experience,
but imagining the real: that's too burdensome, too
wrapped up in discomforts of the flesh. Only dear
father, your love for your children is vague, I don't
know where to begin tracing the marks of the real.

Who are you? Why am I incapable of empathy? It's
the past we've shared muddily, as in the garden, as
in the weeds you used to rip from earth and ground
harshly, as in the slaps you gave me, for nothing

that a child can understand. And you remain this fog of
explanations to me, I don't understand the structure
of your disaster, and I know I've gotten much from you:
restless in every state. Do I love the land as much as
you do? I keep digging, finding shards of broken glass,

a piece of a stocking, things that are fine to the touch
and cutting: something of shame, maybe a sham, and
maybe I am as unaware of you as you are unaware of me,
an image of troubled trouble: some kid you came close to
taming but never did. You know that I have a household,

constructed of "a wife" and "a daughter" and you
wonder: why not more? Why not bring it home, here
to me, you say, so I can have an aid, a son to endure
and exercise these extensions of resounding sounds,
that are all the very practice of silence!
                        And so I ask
myself, not you father now: do I dare, do I
    dare
        write all this
        in a language you understand?

IV

Dirty Underworld

GRAND

i

This is the world as we know it: everything is big and grand and all-encompassing. How long have we been asleep? Some forty years they say. That's fine. We're awake at this dark moment, and there is nothing to be seen.

ii

The numerous vehicles on the surface, of the surface are moving up and down the block. People show pride, but at the early hours of dawn we all yawn and try to control the drip escaping our nostrils in the cold. We've all heard about the word that started it all. We pass each other's facial gestures, mainly contentment and its opposite. Some people know more than others, and the few that know nothing are the lucky ones. Unknown.

iii

Catch that sound! The imaginary voice shouts in the middle of the street as the sun begins setting its orange sails in the sky. Catch a glimpse of the other world, of the orange before they start taking the sky down. The people who know the secret recipe walk down the street hiding a hand in their pocket. They smile walking down. They bare their white teeth for everyone to marvel at the light and the lies spreading over their faces like the hidden veins of vultures.

iv

Little steps are what they are: steps. We could all trip and tip the side of this boat toward drowning. But we hold tight like birds clutching a branch with their claws in the cold. We shiver convulsively looking less and less like birds.

PRAYER

swiping left and right,
bare genitals,
     and exposed,
assholes   yes—

every truth we pronounce—
some matter for laughter, we
the funny people,
comfortable complainers,
first and
last
to know

anything.

this is the production—
cheap disaster, the one
you get from department
stores,
     the one
     you
unpack after breakfast,
play with for a minute
or two
     and then here
it goes:

in the plastic blue,

another recycling
fantasy—

oh,
big round-thighed fantasy of mine

oh, spread your legs,
make us the play—
and while you're at it,
moan:

loud and louder,
and maybe fake it

tell us
of infinities:
how beautiful, how
mysterious it all is

oh yes
          fantasy

fuck us, and
fuck any effort,
any ability,
in the making

and please,
          let us

kneel together
now, bending

knees,
and let us
pray:

benzos benzos
make me numb

benzos benzos
make me dumb

benzos, please,
make my slow

death

really slow.

ANNIVERSARY

the morning river moved by the wind

making ripples that go on and on
                              fold
after fold:
          waking up against sheets I
think, how boring the male mind can
fantasize and regulate what we've been
taught over and over, the whole tits-
and-ass theory
                    the different positions
compared to a cry:
                         ecstasy sister of
fantasy and them together on couch
rubbing against one another
                         —all poetry
aside—what does the sexual gaze have
to do with anything
                         but anger piling
on anger:
          then death by some sort of
release . . .
          and how come the body can produce

all these "fucking" liquids and where

should this drip
          drop
               lead: can we empty?

one day I'll no longer wear my sexual
identity and I'll lead the body against
all particles
           taking one bone after bone
from their bed of flesh
                        and dropping them
in the pit
           and then you and I

my dear beloved can set

           the whole thing
                    on desire.

LOVE POEM

I wanted to write a love poem but instead
I watched the news: there is talk of Syria falling
there is talk of Syria rising, there is only talk

and talk, of a lion griping, fighting, over lots
and lots of talk, though you do remember clearly
that I always wanted you, though we had

no plans for nothing, there were tides and lands
in tides, and incessant talk of nothing, and a
seed to plant in hand, though we've seen it

all in burning, have we not the winds to blame,
yet there is always talk of Syria, there is always
talk of home, and there is always something

eating, there is always something wrong: are
we not too much alike, some sensitive meek
and strong, have we not stuck together, have

we not against the winds: yes there is something
nearing eating, and so what, we've gotten it
all wrong, but I do remember you, and I do

remember me, and I do remember having, our
daughter called the sky, we will walk our steps
pretending that there are always streets to walk

AT THE FARMERS' MARKET

So I've been running on empty for some time, and
now I'm out
    of anger:
Is this the beginning of memory? Who should
I ask? Who should be
    asking?
                      And every-
time I look at the assembly of those market signs
at dawn
    I see my wife and I looking over
      our neighbors' yard
in Indiana, looking over a few men in the dark
as they jump up and down in their truck, waving
Confederate flags and shouting for us to hear:

                Sand Niggers!

Was it in fear we watched, or maybe in some sort
of amazement that we've been summoned here
to take part in this scene, stuck to the edge of a
window as a bunch of guys in the middle of nowhere
exercise something American in my mind, and I'm
thinking, how impressed I am with them having
done their homework on our names, having put

            the two together.

Now the farmers begin to drive in their trucks, begin
setting up their tents, and the stands begin opening
up, and for what:
       This fresh produce,
                 as the Amish man, long
               in his
beard, looks at me, looks right into my eyes as I eye
a speaker beside me, who is also me, speaking in some
language, a tongue sustains him as he describes how
this tomato will be chopped into the mix of colors—
the ones murmuring in a salad bowl:

    Respect and the preservation of difference
              for the greater taste of course!

AT THE POST OFFICE

What was I mailing that day . . . nothing of importance, just bills. I had a few
    of them, not all of
        them were without stamps.

I stood in line eyeing the surroundings. Some services were relabeled, they are
    no longer
        what they were called:

And what inspired the change? I don't know but I cared to know. Maybe an
    attempt at
        clarification, a desire to eliminate

confusion. The more the relabeling will eliminate, the more smoothly things
    go at that window
        up there.

Wishful thinking one might say, and I'd say it's child's play . . . let them do
    whatever keeps them
        busy, as I'm still

standing in line, marveling with red eyes at the "Priority Packages." Some of
    them go by weight,
        some go by

shape: "You Fit It, We Ship It!" one label says. I imagine hands trying to fit
    some malleable thing
        into a box,

the edges of that thing always sticking out. And the hands hurry to control
 that corner while
  another one goes

up, and so on and so forth, till I try hard controlling my imagination as I'm
 still standing, getting
  a bit nervous

for no particular reason. And, of course, you can't tell the mind what to do,
 and the thing turns into
  an octopus

in my bag, and I see myself going a bit mad, trying to get its many legs in there,
 in that box. Oh my
  god, when is this going

to end? The person in front of me wants to mail a package to China. He asks
 where on the
  package, where

should he write in his language? A heated discussion begins to warm up in my
 ear. But none of
  it actually takes

place. The lady points to one corner and simply says, "Here." And to top it off,
 she tells the man
  not to get back

in line: "When you're done just come right up!" And I get called from behind.
 "It's your turn."
  That is stop staring at things

like a good little boy, and let's move this experience a foot and some inches
    ahead. I go up
        myself, I look at the lady

behind the transparent plastic separating us. She looks a bit of a blur to me.
    Her voice seeps
        from the cracks, from

the holes in fake glass, asking me, "What can I do for you?" And I wasn't
    myself then, I looked
        at her blankly and said

almost shouting, "Stamps!" She looked at me without much surprise, as
    though it was expected
        of me to shout. It's all

thought, all of it in my head . . . these scenarios. The lady kindly pointed to
    booklets of stamps.
        "Some food for thought!" I said pointing to a set

with Spanish words, labeling various Mexican meals. And she found what I
    said funny, she really
        smiled. There was

a set of purple hearts, another with the American flag, and there . . . that one
    I've been trying to
        avoid: a picture of an old

woman, a hand being reached to her from behind, touching the shoulder—I
    really couldn't
        believe it—the label

"Alzheimer's" written over in big white letters. I hesitated. I took only the
Mexican food one.
    "That's it?" the nice lady said

as though nothing was. And I said, "I'll take one of those too, the
'Alzheimer's' set," and I
        stuck them in my bag, then picked

up my daughter from school, and I almost forgot, but then I remembered,
and I said to her,
        all in Arabic, of course, let me show you some

stamps. And when seeing "the stamp" she couldn't believe it herself. "That's
grandma!" she
        said, ripping the booklet in half. She

wanted to keep her half, to my surprise! And when it was time to say good
night and goodbye
        as I was going to New York,

she said, "Wait!" She got out of bed, "Her usual trick of not going to sleep," I
thought. She said, "I
        want to give you something,"

she went to her closet of toys, got the booklet out of a drawer of dolls, and
was having trouble
        pulling one of the

stamps out. I reached to help. But it was unnecessary. She did it herself,
ripped part of the
        woman's hair off too, though

not too much, just a little off the top of it, and was sticking it on a piece of
    paper. I was about to
        thank her, but the operation

wasn't done I guess. She said, "Wait!" again, and went to some picture on the
    wall, and started
        ripping something else.

And I was about to get irritated, raised my voice a bit. But she didn't care.
    She said, "Just wait!"
        and went right to

it: a little heart was being ripped off the wall. She stuck it on the back of the
    same paper with
        the stamp, and handed me something

I wasn't sure how to take.

FIVE HOURS, AN AUTOBIOGRAPHY

i

it's this day   mother's birthday   and what is she   now
mother   her body   her ghost   I'm trying to think
only of her   to separate   the whole of her   her name   *nawal*
from all   and what to say   just what is said

and what to remember?   she was she is   a bit   out of her mind
some kindness she possessed   the kind that makes you   made her
bitter I guess   and I know and that's what I would   say
and that's what I will   remember   remember

and this is what she said   the night before   our trip to Amman
to my second attempt   at settling in some thought   to America
an engineer   mining the machine   minding his own design
leaving all poetry behind   and then she spoke   she said   don't go off

studying the mechanics of machines   philosophize   do a thing
of the mind   she said she knew   she spoke at last   why now
why didn't she say a word before   always late   in her pronouncements
and then off we went   sleep never abandoning   us the sleepless

to the bridge   the sun was out   to the entire structure   from
van to bus   from search to search   guns and all   we face
we call it   bridge *jisr*   and there wasn't a thing laughable about it
and we didn't laugh   just us two   after I had gone before   on my own

these were different times   they gave me a permit then   at that time
I flew out of Tel Aviv   the permit takes you straight   there   no
right or left   my first trip to *Israel*   was straight   to the airport
and never again   that was the beginning   the end

back to bridge   uprising for the second time   to the U.S.   another
attempt   at settling in some thought   my father didn't let me stay   you see
what's become of this place he said   you have to finish   what you've
begun   see the bullets and holes   this door   yes   then I'll become

whatever times demand   an engineer   so dear to his words
it'll never work   she said   her honesty shocked me in   that night
and her silence didn't comfort much at day   and together we rode
to the bridge   her lips moving without a sound   mincing her words again.

ii
in the big waiting hall   people line up   here and there   I stay
with her   she goes first   her passport   stamped   she was ready
go   behind the glass separating me   a man in a box   I wait
I see him   coming out   taking my passport   with him

somewhere   I didn't understand   I remained   where I was
eyeing what I see of a chair in a wooden box   looking around   he comes
back   stops at his little door   exchanges a laugh with a passing figure   haha
he enters the box   sits down on a chair   he says to me   in some language

I can't remember   what was it   he did speak   he did point
to where   the place I need to go   in Hebrew in Arabic   in some gesture that said
you go   you wait   there   pointing to another line   people
that side of the hall   against a white waiting wall   that I never   bothered to see.

iii
and where did she go   mother?

78

iv

ten years after   I met with him   the uncle who drove us   mother and I
to the airport in Amman   and he said   your mother didn't fall   silent   after
we dropped you off   this is how she felt   she blamed your father for it
she said   he drove you all   away   as she saw   another son go

I didn't care to ask   did she go back to the bridge   that day   that night
how could she have gone through   how could she   on her own   after I was
taken and held   in a room   some five hours   didn't know where she
was   didn't know how she passed the time   and still   I don't

why did we not   communicate   dramatize   and over   five hours
nothing really going on   just people going in and out   to where
god only knows   who cares   I just remained   with another man and we
didn't speak   we were in such a space   no words   and just like that

we were let go   five hours for us to remember   and never to forget
my mother still in the hall   waiting   oh god   she looked pale
her lips looked dry   but she was fine   she said   *al hamdu li llah*   let's
go   yes thank god   we did   but never did we   never did she

forget.

v

did I tell her the rest   the story then I might've never did   after she and my uncle
left   after that goodbye in Amman   another airport   after we were ready   to end all
drama after that   yes   a Jordanian officer   border-control again   checking
didn't let me through   this is not real he said   your visa   a fabrication

and what did I say   I didn't say I stood   there   fumbling for proofs
bringing them out of a bag   placing them in front of eyes   no glass there separating
us   and there   no confusion   no conclusion   either
the language we spoke   little did I know   he wanted a bribe   I didn't

at that age   he didn't budge   little did I know   I raised a voice   my only proof
said something rude *leave it to them*   *the americans who issued it*   *they'll say   who*
are you   another officer came   and I don't know how   I ended
up   on an escalator   carrying   mother's heavy load

of seeds and weeds   all sorts of foods   dry and dead   she stuck
in a carry-on   for me   to keep and remember   this home this land
and on the ascending steps I paused   there   for a bit of breath   some strength
and maybe to look back   at the doors leading out   and maybe to see   and maybe

to say   may you   my mother   be there   there   somewhere.

MALMOUM

Don't waste a line, your ink, or anything
        else:

there's no room for all the thinking of you
        and others

on this page: you are you, you are not
        you, as one

ancient poet put it for mouths to repeat
        after him

for how many years? And there is the look-
        out, for your

spring Abu Tammam—your word is one
        with the world

too often: you are the true discovery of
        exile—the self

wanders and adopts you, only to remain
        in you, intact,

thank god! There is still a possible thing,
        there is, still

the stone, standing, brushing again and
        again, against

the accidents of the world and there that
    word, and the

sound, its echo that keeps us all together
    and very much

lonely.

EPILOGUE: ANOTHER TONGUE SUSTAINS YOU

*

I've been telling this story now, over
and over, as an application of identity:
that language meant nothing to me as
a child, till I heard it being put to form:

that the sounds were inescapable
as father disappeared pronouncing
ancient verses in the guest room, under-
neath the yellow bulb hanging from

above: I was probably three or four, and
I began picking up something, not words,
not language, but the Arabic of then
and now the one frozen in books:

and there, a picture of me on a stage
with longish black-brown hair, a face
in the site of dim lights, lips parting as
if to say, as I'm about to say, though shying:

I'm dressed in a brown corduroy suit,
raising a hand in the air, I'm five now,
first grade perhaps, I've been hearing
verses read aloud, and now I'm reciting:

lines of poetry, there in the openness,
in front of everyone, before the entire
school, before the war,
                    and this beginning

of spring
      shuts us all down.

         *

And the line tells us: *stop, stand*

Up—should we cry?

The memory of loved ones,

The specific places of the heart,

The one shaped and

Shaping . . .

A self in you:

    The balcony, facing
Southeast,
      Where you played
Beating the carpets
Clean,

    The flat roof
Of the house, the one
With the iron rods sticking
Out,
      And the lines of tar
      Burning
Your hands:
      The garlic
Hanging by the wall
Of that room   the one

With the railings
Leafing   all the way
To the west you can
See   that stretch of land
And the olive tree hidden behind
A shed
        This is where I used
To hide and this where
I still am.

                    *

Now nothing comforting about the world—
        I keep putting off   the tongue
insisting on a language
                        far off, even
in a dream, and I keep telling
and retelling my daughter to repeat
her sentences

        in Arabic.

But history can't get us to comprehend
now:
        What language is language?
I talk this Arabic as much as I can
but there is no use, the moments

you create are all in the past, and the
progression as you well know by now
is disastrous:
        The theoretical matters
of living remain intact, indeed I see.

NOTES

"*Jisr*": *Jisr* is the Arabic word for bridge, but Palestinians use the word to refer to the entire border-control structure and the process by which they cross from Palestine and the "West Bank" to Jordan or vice versa.

"Lines of Return": I make a reference to the poet Abu Tammam, using his opening line "You are not you and home is not home." I also borrow some phrasing from Tom Sleigh's poem "House of Fact, House of Ruin." Additionally, the wording "at the sight of ruins, stop" is a reference to the opening motif common in classical Arabic poetry.

"House Cleaning": I borrow the line "my mother my mother my mother she" from Ellen Bryant Voigt's poem "My Mother."

"Love Poem": The reference to the lion is a play on the Arabic name Asad, which literally means "lion."

"*Malmoum*": The title and the reference to the stone are taken from a verse by the poet Ibn Muqbil.

"Epilogue: Another Tongue Sustains You": The phrases in italics are loosely taken from the Arabic of the *Mu'allaqah* by the poet Imru' al-Qays.